GAINING
COOPERATION
For the Workers' Comp Professional

3 Easy Steps to Getting Injured Workers
To Do What You Want Them To Do

By CARL VAN AND DEBRA HINZ

INTERNATIONAL INSURANCE INSTITUTE, INC.

Written by Carl van Lamsweerde and Debra Hinz

Book cover design by Patton Brothers Illustration & Design, Inc.
Interior layout by Ann van Lamsweerde
Edited by Karla Alcerro

First Edition

Copyright ©2011 International Insurance Institute, Inc. 2112
Belle Chasse Hwy. #11-¬319, Gretna, LA 70056   T:504-393-4570
888-414-8811

www.InsuranceInstitute.com
www.ClaimsProfessionalBooks.com

Published by International Insurance Institute, Inc.

ISBN: 1461104009
ISBN-13: 9781461104001

Printed in Charleston, SC.

Dedication

For my lost family members: my father Franz van Lamsweerde, my mother Joyce Martin, my brother Lex van Lamsweerde, my uncle Leon Martin, my uncle Mac Stephens, my uncle Leo van Lamsweerde, my cousin Peter Martin, my father-in-law Dick Wimsatt, all my grandparents, and my friend and brother-in-law Robert Wimsatt.

-Carl Van

To all my friends in the Worker's Comp Industry, thank you for your friendship and support; I hope you enjoy the information within these pages.

-Debra Hinz

Acknowledgements

We would like to take just a moment to acknowledge some of our Workers' Comp friends who have supported our efforts to help improve the Workers Comp industry, and also to some who contributed concepts to this book.

Diann Cohen, Rebecca Hughes – Macro Pro
Peter Strauss, Rick Duane – Montana State Fund
Jim Greer – AE21
Jill Benner, Media Oakley – CEU Institute
Scott Marshall, Deirdre Millwood, Sandy Hodge - American Claims Management
Kristi Bowen - Avizent Risk
Deborah Desuyo , Julie Wetzel- Berkshire Hathaway
Jennifer Smith, Sabrina Darsey - Corvel
John Riggs - Disney Corporation
Kit Mu - Intercare
Brenda Calvert, Erin Orr, Lesley Kochel - Sedgwick CMS
Karen Parker - The Zenith
Marlon Mendosa - Tower Insurance
Cheryl Gray - Majestic Insurance
John Meier - Employers Resources Northwest (ERNWest)
Dianna Cumpian, Tana Chicarelli, Sarah Winslow,
        Melissa Scherer, Debbie Danesh – Gallagher Bassett
Tiffany Zidenberg - Apex
Amy Hand – Pinnacol Insurance
Karel Davis – State Comp Insurance Fund

Thank You

Thank You

To my daughter Amanda van Lamsweerde (soon to be Ph.D.) who keeps teaching me how the brain really works. – Carl Van

To Patty Waldeck and Chip Payne- Just because….To Carl Van- for allowing me to be a part of this project. To Tiffany Zidenberg...friend extraordinaire! – Debra Hinz

Special Thanks

As always, a special thanks to my father, John Martin. Who not only continues to support all of my business efforts, but having raised me with a desire to help others, continues to support me with his invaluable guidance whenever I need it. – Carl Van

Diann Cohen, my twin sister, who collaborates, brain storms and inspires me daily. – Debra Hinz

Very Special Thanks

Very special thanks to my beautiful wife, Ann van Lamsweerde, who is always there for me. Not only is she supportive, but she has the greatest inner strength of anyone I have ever known. Despite difficult times, the murder of her brother and hurricane Katrina, she remains kind, generous and always gracious. I admire her beyond words. – Carl Van

Very special thanks to Paul and Michael Hinz for making my life fun. – Debra Hinz

About the Authors

Carl Van was born Carl Christian Gregory Maria Baron van Lamsweerde. He was the second son of a prominent Dutch noble and artist, Franciscus Ludovicus Aloysius Maria Baron van Lamsweerde.

After the death of Carl's father at the age of 11, his mother, Joyce, married John E. Martin. Mr. Martin was a successful business owner and investor. Mr. Martin had tremendous influence over Carl, recapping stories of coming to America with virtually nothing and building a successful business. Carl admired his new father greatly, and marveled at his generosity.

Carl had a remarkable resemblance to his father Franz, and was greatly influenced by John. His mother would often comment, "I look at Carl and I see Franz. Then he starts to talk, and out comes John."

Carl worked his way through college, taking years of night school to earn his degree in Insurance. By the time he earned his degree, Carl was already a

Regional Claims Manager, and even writing and teaching several IEA courses.

With his first marriage, came his daughter Amanda Elaine Denise Baroness van Lamsweerde, who Carl continuously proclaims is a child genius.

Carl married Ann Elizabeth Wimsatt, on July 16, 1994, and together they have lived in Sacramento, CA, Nashville, TN, and now reside in New Orleans, LA. In April of 1998, Carl sold his house, cashed in his retirement, and gambled it all on the idea that insurance companies would be interested in meaningful, real-life claims training. He created International Insurance Institute, Inc. a company dedicated to the enhancement of the insurance claims industry, and now widely considered the single best claims training company in the United States and Canada.

Carl Van has dedicated his life to studying how people think and interact, and has developed classes and programs to improve the success of individuals as well business groups.

I have known Carl since we met in kindergarten, and even back then in our school days. Carl looked out for people. Obviously, Carl was honing his skills that he uses today. It only takes a few minutes in his presence to know how passionately he believes that the greatest thing a person can do in this life, is be of service to someone in need. That, he insists, is the opportunity most of us have every single day.

In this book, as with all of his materials, Carl shares his wit, wisdom, knowledge and sixth sense of dealing with people. He's a great friend and an inspiration. I hope you find this book as valuable in your world as Carl has been in mine.

-Steve Belkin, Open All Nite Entertainment.

Debra Hinz was born Debra Diann Feltman in Everett Washington. Her mother, Theresia Reygers survived the harsh conditions of WWII as a young girl in Indonesia when her family was placed into a concentration camp. She taught Debra many skills including being resourceful, living to a high standard and never settling for mediocrity. Debra's father, Palmer Feltman, an American serviceman, taught Debra the value of service to others, the structure of business and the need for personal goals. Together they set the stage for Debra's worldwide travels and accomplishments.

Debra began her sales career early and was quickly promoted to Vice President for Continental Lawyers. Her attention to customer satisfaction proved to be a key element to her success and remains a guiding principle. She learned that effective sales and marketing depends on a quality product and great customer service.

Debra is always quick to help others. A good example of this is when soon after arriving to Adana, Turkey, Debra attended an officer wives' function. It was mostly US Air Force officer wives; however, Debra noticed a Turkish woman to whom no one seemed to be paying attention. Debra spent the evening making her feel welcome and ensuring she had an enjoyable time. The next day the Turkish commander came to Debra's door to thank her. It turns out this woman was the Turkish commander's wife, and so Debra and her family became fast friends with their family.

Years later this story made its way to both the Governor of California and the former Vice President of the United States who both asked Debra to recount the tale.

In 2001, Debra entered the workers' compensation field with Macro-Pro Copy and Subpoena Services, determined to improve the quality of services available to examiners. By 2002, she realized there was a need for quality Continuing Education training for examiners and service providers. She formed the Association of Insurance Professionals, which became an instant success and continues to be the largest attended workers' comp association in California.

Debra has also been a member of several association boards and committees, providing keen details on how they can improve their effectiveness by focusing on the needs of the attendees.

Debra's core values have her focusing on people instead of policies, on customer care before personal goals, and on developing relationships instead of getting lost in the details. Debra's broad experience in the industry and her unique talent at building trust, has contributed to her ability to help others succeed and ultimately to her own great success.

With over 20 years of leadership roles in the insurance industry, Debra has developed insightful methodologies for customer management and relationship development.

I hope you enjoy the insight she lends to this book.

-Cathy Aguilar
Workers' Compensation Claims Manager
California Self Insured Security Fund

Table of Contents

Dedication iii

Acknowledgements v

Thanks and Special Thanks vii

About the Author ix

Chapter Song References xvii

Introduction xix

Chapter 1   Hammer Time 25

Chapter 2   Help! 31

Chapter 3   Hammer Time Revisited 37

Chapter 4   Everything You Know is Wrong. 45

Chapter 5   Don't Want to Fight 51

Chapter 6   Not Some Monster 59

Chapter 7   Trust Abounding 73

Summary   Here's Where the Story Ends 79

Chapter Song References

Song	Performer	Album	Written By
Be Our Guest	Angela Lansbury	Beauty and the Beast	Howard Ashman, Tim Rice
U Can't Touch This	M.C. Hammer	Please Hammer, Don't Hurt 'Em	Stanley Kirk Burrell, Alonzo Miller, Rick James
Help!	The Beatles	Help!	John Lennon, Paul McCartney
El Condor Pasa	Simon and Garfunkel	Bridge Over Troubled Water	Daniel Alomía Robles Jorge Milchberg, Paul Simon
Everything You Know is Wrong	Weird Al Yankovic	Bad Hair Day	Weird Al Yankovic
It's a Little Bit Me, It's a Little Bit You	The Monkeys	Monkeemania	Neil Diamond
The Ballad of the Kingsmen	Todd Snider	East Nashville Skyline	Todd Snider
The Age of Aquarius	The 5th Dimension	From Musical "Hair"	Gerome Ragni, James Rado, Galt MacDermot
Here's Where the Story Ends	The Sundays	Reading, Writing and Arithmetic	Harriet Wheeler

Be Our Guest

Be our guest. Be our guest.
Put our service to the test!

"Be Our Guest" – Angela Lansbury (Beauty and the Beast)

We would like you to be our guest on this journey into gaining cooperation. We consider ourselves trainers, course designers, and coaches . . . not writers. So please, forgive us if during this book, we slip in and out of our trainer mode and; instead of just commenting on what Awesome Examiners do, we actually try to teach. Just be glad we don't have a flip chart.

We prefer to talk to people rather than to write to them. We love the phone and hate e-mail. This is why we have chosen to write this book in a style, as if we are talking to someone. We will refer to you, the reader, of this book without having any idea who you are or what you do. That is to simply help us convey the concepts without tuning out. It helps us if we pretend we're talking to someone rather than writing to them.

We mention this because we wouldn't want anyone to get mad at us and say to themselves, "What are they talking about, I don't do that." Just know that when we refer to "you," we're talking to those of you who see the need for improvement and want help.

We freely use the word "we" throughout this book, because we want you to know we are on your side. After all, we are not writing this book for only the upper echelon of management. We are writing it for those of us who are on the front lines. So we hope nobody minds that we fight to stay in the club.

Another thing you should know when reading this book, is that in most cases when we use names for customers and employees, that those are not the actual names of those employees and/or customers. They are the names of friends and family members. We decided this might increase the chance that someone might read this book if they knew their name was in it.

However, when we refer to actual Awesome Employees and use first and last name, rest assured that these people are real, and are out there right now being awesome. Some have since moved into management, and others love their jobs so much they stay right where they are.

Admission #1: We are not researchers. You should know that we did not conduct formal research. We have no control groups to test out our theories, and no written documentation to substantiate each and every hypothesis. However, we did receive a great deal of assistance from some fine people in the workers' comp community.

What we do offer is practical experience and examples to better qualify how to gain cooperation. After our combined 50+ years in the business world, years of management and executive experience, 15+ years of monitoring phone calls, designing training programs, and facilitating over 1,000 workshops, we have a certain perspective about what one can do to gain cooperation. That is what we are relying upon, so don't expect to find us in some Management Journal. We're not there. We're here, trying to help.

Admission #2: Carl is Lazy. (Probably has something to do with Admission #1) Carl's first book, _The 8 Characteristics of the Awesome Adjuster_, was quite successful in the claims world. Ever since its release, he has been bombarded with people telling him the skills, characteristics, and attitudes that make great claims people mentioned in the book are completely transferable to almost any industry. After years of people telling him that he should rewrite it with a more general outlook, he finally agreed. That book is called, _The 8 Characteristics of the Awesome Employee._ He is in negotiations with several U.S. publishing companies currently for the rights. Look for it soon!

He dedicated quite a large section of that book to gaining cooperation, and he decided to give that information its own platform, and published a book for the general public entitled, _Gaining Cooperation: Some Easy Steps to Getting Customers to do What You Want Them to do._ When that came out, we heard nothing but requests from various lines of business in the insurance community to create a version specific to their needs. We decided to start with Workers' Comp, and so now we have <u>this</u> book. Is that lazy or what? Yes, the information is the same, the names are the same, and even the titles of the chapters are the same. Lazy!

Admission #3: We have terrible memories. We want to tell you that <u>every single</u> story we tell in the book, things we have witnessed, things people have said to us are absolutely true!

Well, mostly true. Probably all except two...MAYBE three. Which three? We're not telling you. You see, although we have every intention of telling the truth, or at least how we remember things, we don't intend on sitting on The Daily Show or The Today Show someday trying to justify every little detail. This way, if we're caught exaggerating, or challenged by one of our previous managers that we make fun of, we can just say, "That's one of the three."

Admission #4: We hate being sued. So, throughout this book, we are going to refer to people by name. Sometimes they're real people with their real names or real people and with fake names. Sometimes, we might even make up a fake person and a fake name.

We might be telling a story from a prior article, book, magazine, or even video presentation. We might tell the exact same story but with two different people's names. The reason for that is very simple. Sometimes we use fake names because we don't want to get sued. Would you want to get sued? No, of course you wouldn't. And neither do we. If we do make any money off of this book, we certainly don't want to spend it in legal fees defending ourselves against some idiot because we've used his real name in a book. So, for the most part, we will probably be using fake names.

However, there will be times when we use real people and their real names. Those times will probably be when we give you both their first and last name. So when we refer to someone by their whole name, you can be assured that these people really exist and the stories are somewhat accurate, at least to the best of our memory.

So, if you happen to read an article either one of us wrote a number of years ago and we are telling a story and we use a different person's name, don't get your undies in a bunch. It's just what we do. We just like to use names because referring to people as "my manager," "my co-worker," "my partner," all the time can become a little monotonous. So just bear with us and come along for the ride.

CHAPTER 1

Hammer Time

Stop….Hammer time!

"U Can't Touch This" – MC Hammer

Before we can discuss the right way to be persuasive, we must rule out the wrong way to be persuasive, and that is what we will refer to as "the cooperation hammer."

The Cooperation Hammer

As workers' compensation professionals, we constantly need to gain cooperation from the injured workers and service providers with whom we work. Some people in their particular disciplines don't need to work too hard in order to gain cooperation from people. Grocery store clerks, for example, don't need to convince customers that they need to go pick out their items and bring them to him/her. They don't need to convince the customer that they need to take the items out of the basket and put them on the belt to be scanned. They don't need to convince anyone that when they ring up the total they should pay for it.

A grocery store clerk may, however, have to convince a customer that the coupons that they are using aren't the right ones. Or that just because an item is mispriced, doesn't mean the customer is entitled to get the item for that price, or a number of other things.

Workers' compensation examiners, however, require a good bit of convincing skills in their daily work. An examiner might need to convince an injured worker that they have to fill out a medical release form in order to determine the value of their claim. Or they might have to convince an injured worker to complete a medical evaluation form in order to be seen by a doctor. Or they might have to convince an injured worker to see the doctor in order to continue with their benefits. There are many examples of when an examiner will have to convince someone to cooperate with them.

Examiners spend a fair amount of time just negotiating for cooperation: Trying to convince an injured worker to fill out a form, sign an authorization or to sign a release. Unfortunately, some examiners go about the process the opposite way that it is most effective. More often, they pull out the "cooperation hammer."

The cooperation hammer is the tool most often used to convince someone to cooperate. The objective is to inflict so much pain that there is no way the injured worker can resist, and ultimately they do what is demanded of them.

Let's look at an example where "Suzanne," a workers' compensation examiner is trying to get her injured worker, "Mr. Wimsatt," to complete a required form. The conversation might go like this:

> Suzanne: *Mr. Wimsatt, in order for me to continue your disability benefits, you need to complete the form I sent you and send it back to me.*

> Mr. Wimsatt: *I'm not doing that, no way.*

> Suzanne: *Well if you don't, there's no way I can continue your benefits.* (Whack!)

The approach by Suzanne, in order to gain cooperation from Mr. Wimsatt, is to pull out the cooperation hammer and start whacking away. You might ask yourself, "Why is this the wrong tool? It works." People do cooperate when we inflict pain on them. The problem with the cooperation hammer is not that it doesn't work; the problem is that it works just fine.

We can inflict pain on the injured worker so they co-operate with us. However, once you gain cooperation by inflicting pain on an injured worker, all you have now is an angry person who's going to try to get back at you at every turn. It's going to be why they don't cooperate with you, it's going to be why they question everything you do, it's why they're going to challenge everything that you say. Because you pushed them into doing something they didn't want to do, because you could, because you are stronger than they are. You just darn well proved it to them.

What is this cooperation hammer we love to pull out? Well, usually it is the facts. We love to hit people with the facts. We do it all the time. Do any of these sound familiar: "If you won't sign this release, we can't get the medical records to determine the value of your claim" (Whack) "If you do not treat within the Medical Provider Network we will deny your treatment." (Whack)

"If you do not return my call, I cannot obtain infor-mation to determine if your claim is compensable." (Whack)

We use force because we are stronger than they are, and we have a big cooperation hammer, which we use to whack them until they can't take the pain any-more. They finally do what we asked them to do. But, we now have a built-in enemy.

So how do we help? Start using <u>the</u> word.

CHAPTER 2

Help!

Help. I need somebody.
Help. Not just anybody.
Help. You know I need someone…HELP!

"Help" – The Beatles

A dividing line between truly awesome examiners, and everybody else, is that people who make out-standing examiners are people who use the word "help," a lot. It's in their daily vocabulary.

You see, they actually believe that they are in the business of providing assistance to these people and they care about them. So they use the word help a lot. Instead of saying, "Let me tell you why we did that," they will actually say, "Let me help you under-stand why we do this." Instead of saying, "You are go-ing to have to fill out this form or else we can't pay you," they will say, "If you can fill out the form, I can help you by making sure you get paid." They use the word help a lot.

They don't say, "I have been assigned to handle your claim," they will say, "I am going to be helping you with your claim." The word help seems to slip out very often. And because they use the word help quite a bit, they tend to do a great job with customer service, because people tend to trust someone who is trying to help them.

Let's say you have the entire spectrum of trust. A line with all the things you can do to make someone not trust you on one end and all the things you can do to make someone trust you on the other end.

NO TRUST -----a little-----some-----more-----TRUST

One of the things you can do to make the injured worker completely not trust you, clear on the left side, is threaten them. Give them an ultimatum and see if they ever trust you again. Clear on the right side, to make the person fully trust you, is to offer to help them. You see, most people trust someone who is trying to help them, and they don't trust someone who is trying to threaten them, hurt them, or give them an ultimatum.

Is there a difference between telling someone, "If you don't sign this form we can't pay you" and "If you do sign this form I can help make sure you get paid?" What do you think? Is there a difference between those two statements? One is a threat and an ultimatum, and the other one is an offer to help.

The funny thing about it is sometimes we actually believe we are trying to help the injured worker when we threaten them. We are actually thinking, "I am going to help this person understand that if they don't sign this form they won't get paid." The problem is sometimes it comes off as a threat. So the people who tend to make the best examiners are people who use the word help. A lot! Because they use the word help, they get people to calm down and trust them much more than the average examiner.

Usually, the cooperation hammer will work. However, most often it is not the right tool. Maybe there is another tool that can be used. The tool most awesome examiners pull out, before the cooperation hammer, is the "Why" tool. That's right, a simple one word question, "Why?"

Let's take a look at the value of this tool. Yes…yes, we understand this example is an auto claim and not a workers' comp claim, but since it really happened, we wanted to use it. We believe any claims person can understand what this demonstrates.

Pat was trying to settle a total loss with a customer. Pat had his array of facts, including a fair market evaluation report completed by a company called CCC.

It showed the value of the customer's vehicle to be about $12,500. Pat called up the customer, and here is how the conversation went:

Pat: *Mr. Blasz, I have the fair market evaluation back on your car and it turns out that your car is worth $12,500. We'd like to pay you $12,500 to settle your claim.*

Mr. Blasz: *No, I really feel my car is worth $13,000.*

Pat: *Well, I have a CCC report that says it's worth $12,500.* (Whack!)

Mr. Blasz: *Well, I still feel my car is worth $13,000.*

Pat: *Mr. Blasz, you know if you don't take the $12,500, we can't pay the storage charges on your car anymore.* (Whack!)

Mr. Blasz: *Look, I understand, but I still feel my car is worth $13,000.*

Pat: *If we don't settle this today, we're not going to be able to pay for your rental car any longer either.* (Whack!)

Mr. Blasz: *Look, like I said, I really feel my car is worth $13,000.*

Pat: *Okay, but if you don't take the offer, you're still going to have to make your car payment.* (Whack!)

Of course listening to this, it is obvious that Pat was going to have a difficult time settling this case, which he didn't do in that conversation. What Pat doesn't know, is that if he changed his process just a little, he could have settled this case. See, Pat's trying to convince this person to give in. It's much easier to convince someone you're right, than it is to get them to give in if they think you're wrong.

When Pat was confronted with the fact that he didn't settle the case, Pat shrugged his shoulders and said, "Ahh, he'll get tired of walking."

You know what? Pat was right, that customer did get tired of walking. In a week, he called and said, "Fine I'll take your stupid $12,500." In the meantime, he may have trashed the company's name all over the place, called up three times to make complaints, and caused a tremendous amount of time and trouble for Pat. The cooperation hammer will work; it'll work just fine. But it will take a lot of time to inflict so much pain on the person before they finally give in, that it's a big time–waster and a very big loss of customer service resources.

Guess what question Pat never asked the customer, not one single time? That's right, he never asked him "Why?" He never said, "Why do you feel your car is worth $13,000?"

Pat never asked "Why?" because he has his cooperation hammer and it works just fine. Why does he care what the customer's reasons are? He's going to win this fight. He's got his cooperation hammer, and he will whack away at this customer until the customer surrenders. And when the customer does, Pat will think to himself, "Man, am I ever a good negotiator!"

As you read this, let me ask you, are you curious why this customer wanted $13,000? Well, guess what, he was asked as part of a follow-up customer service call.

When asked, "By the way, why do you feel your car is worth $13,000?" You know what he said? The answer to that question had nothing to do with any CCC fair market evaluation report. It had nothing to do with car payments. It had nothing to do with storage charges. And it certainly had nothing to do with him staying in a rental car.

The reason this customer wanted $13,000 for his car had absolutely <u>nothing</u> to do with what Pat was literally beating him to death with. Pat just didn't know it because he didn't pull out the right tool; he never asked why.

CHAPTER 3

Hammer Time Revisited

I'd rather be a hammer than a nail

"El Condor Pasa" – Simon and Garfunkel

STEPS TO GAINING COOPERATION:	1. WHY
	2.
	3.

So what did Pat pull out? He pulled out his cooperation hammer and started whacking away. He knew that in a week, Mr. Blasz would settle this case and he would feel like he did a good job. The downfall is, he's taken far more time than he would have had to if he had instead pulled out the right tool. He could have pulled out "Why?" but he didn't.

Do you know what this customer said when asked why he wanted $13,000? He said, "Look, my brother gave me that car and he died about six months ago. It's all I have from him. And I know someone had recently offered him $13,000 for it, and I'm not going to let you guys rip him off."

Can you imagine the feelings this customer had wrapped up into this car? Do you think there was any way this customer was going to be swayed by storage charges? Think about it. If this customer did accept anything less than $13,000, then he would be letting an insurance company rip off his dead brother. Is this customer going to be convinced by rental charges? Is he going to give in because Pat brought up car payments? Of course not. Pat would never know that because he simply never asked "Why?" He had his cooperation hammer, and he used it.

There's an old saying and it goes like this: "When all you have is a hammer, everything looks like a nail." From Abraham Maslow, *The Psychology of Science*, 1966. Guess what that means. It's very simple. It doesn't matter if you need a saw, it doesn't matter if you need a pair of pliers, and it certainly doesn't matter if you need sand paper. If all you have is a hammer, you're going to use it, even if it's the wrong tool. Why, because it's all you've got. And what do you do with a hammer? You hit things with it.

Often times we try to convince other people to do what we want by pulling out the cooperation hammer and inflicting pain on them. We don't literally mean to cause them pain, but in effect that's what it does. By telling someone what will happen to them if they don't do what we ask them, we are inflicting pain upon that person.

We would like to submit that telling someone, "Here's how this will hurt you if you don't do this" will get a different reaction than, "Here's how this will help you if you do this." These are two completely different things. They both gain cooperation, but one doesn't start a war like the other one does.

Funny thing with the "Why?" tool is that even if we ask the other person why, we often still resort to our pounding away with the cooperation hammer. Let's return to that original conversation where the examiner wanted the injured worker to complete the medical release form. Here is how the call might go:

> Suzanne: *Mr. Wimsatt, in order for me to continue your disability benefits, you need to complete the form I sent you and send it back to me.*
>
> Mr. Wimsatt: *I'm not doing that, no way.*
>
> Suzanne: *Well if you don't, there's no way I can continue your benefits.* (Whack!)
>
> Mr. Wimsatt: *Look, I'm not going to fill out the form.*

Suzanne: *Why not?*

Mr. Wimsatt: *Because I'm tired of you guys making me jump through hoops. Why should I run around doing your job? I'm the one who got injured. I'm the victim.*

Suzanne: *Mr. Wimsatt, it's not my job to fill out the form for you. If you want your benefits, you're going to have to fill out the form I sent you and send it back to me. (Whack!)*

Mr. Wimsatt: *I'm not doing it.*

Suzanne: *Why not?*

Mr. Wimsatt: *I told you why!*

Suzanne: *Well if you don't, I can't continue your benefits. (Whack!)*

Notice a couple of things. The first is that the examiner finally did pull out their "Why?" tool, but only after annoying the injured worker. First she gave him a nice big whack with her cooperation hammer, before even bothering to ask why. Most of the time, eventually we will ask the person who is not cooperating why. Unfortunately, it's not our first response, our first response is to give them a nice big whack with our cooperation hammer and then if it occurs to us, we will finally ask "Why?" But by that time, the argument process has already begun.

Notice a second thing, after the examiner asked why, she went right back to using the cooperation hammer.

Based on monitored phone calls, we firmly believe that most arguments are started when an examiner mishears what was just said in a conversation. You may disagree with this statement, because we haven't provided you with enough evidence to convince you, but perhaps by the end of this book we will. However, we wanted to bring up this point just to lay the groundwork.

Most often, the argument begins when an examiner doesn't listen to a statement the injured worker has just made. Most arguments could be completely avoided if both parties actually heard what the other person was saying.

Take the example above. When Suzanne finally does ask why, Mr. Wimsatt told her why, which is what Suzanne reacted to. Suzanne reacted to what she thought she heard, which is "Why should I do your job?" Unfortunately, what she didn't hear was that Mr. Wimsatt just called himself a victim. This guy used the word victim to describe himself.

Mr. Wimsatt said, "Why should I run around doing your job? I'm the one who got injured. I'm the victim." The key words were not the question about the job, which is what Suzanne heard, but the fact that the injured worker called himself a victim.

While listening to this conversation, right away it was rather obvious this person was clearly saying why he wouldn't cooperate. He used the word victim to describe himself. What do we normally associate the word victim with? Usually, it's associated with a crime of some sort. This person is using the same word that he might use to describe himself in the event he was held up or robbed or attacked in some way. He is using the word "victim" to describe himself.

And the funny thing about it is he's perfectly justified in feeling that way. The way he sees it, he has to jump through hoops and waste his time and complete the form, when he's the one who got injured and who's being inconvenienced. None of this is fair and for him to feel like a victim is perfectly reasonable. The problem is the examiner didn't hear that, she instead heard, "Why should I have to run around doing your job?"

What should have been that examiner's response? Well, even if she had heard the injured worker using the word victim, she likely still would have pulled out her cooperation hammer as we all would and now try to convince the person that he is wrong about being a victim. We are going to try to convince them that they are wrong for the way they feel. And we are going to say something along the lines of, "Oh no, you're not a victim, you shouldn't feel that way."

Can you ever change the way someone feels by giving them a bunch of facts? It usually doesn't work and it usually makes them feel stupid, and allowing them to now dig in to battle with you over two issues. You are trying to change the way they feel and they don't want to feel stupid.

Most of us do a very good job of listing a bunch of facts, figures, and reasons why someone should change the way they feel. Unfortunately, that doesn't work very well. So why do we use it? Because it's the only tool we have. We don't have any other tool, so we pull out the cooperation hammer and we start whacking away with facts and figures, trying to change the way the other person feels.

The best examiners remember to correctly use the first tool, which is the question why. Now let's look at the second tool that might actually work in changing the way someone feels, "acknowledgement."

CHAPTER 4

Everything You Know is Wrong

Everything you know is wrong. Black is white, up is down and short is long.
And everything you thought was just so important…
doesn't really matter anymore.

"Everything You Know is Wrong" – Weird Al Yankovic

STEPS TO GAINING COOPERATION:	1. WHY 2. ACKNOWLEDGE 3.

For fans of the show "Seinfeld," you will remember an episode where George concludes that every single decision he has ever made and every single approach he took in his past life had been completely wrong. Every gut instinct he had, has always led him to disaster. So he incorporates a new philosophy: if everything that he has ever done was wrong, then the opposite must be right. And from that point forward, instead of doing what he would normally do, he does the exact opposite. Of course things work out very well for him. He gets a new girlfriend, he gets a new job, and his life becomes quite blissful (for a while).

While not suggesting that exact philosophy, but in order to be persuasive we often pull out the cooperation hammer when that is the exact opposite of what we should use. Most of us tend to pull out the cooperation hammer and start whacking away when we are trying to convince the injured worker of our point of view. In fact, we will be very detailed in pointing out why their beliefs are wrong and hitting them with our cooperation hammer so hard that they eventually give in. Keep in mind, whacking does work, but it should not be used because it creates a battle that you don't need to have.

An important theory on negotiation is, "Great negotiators never argue with reasons; they argue the facts!" That's the Grand Theory about Negotiation #1.

Read it again and think about that just for a second. What are we negotiating? We are negotiating for cooperation. And when negotiating for cooperation, the very best negotiators never argue with people's reasons; they argue the facts.

You see, when you argue with someone's reasons, you are trying to prove them wrong. In fact, most of us believe that in order to convince someone we're right, we have to show them that they are wrong.

It is just a natural response for us. It's a kind of "Let me show you that you are wrong so that you will see that I am right" impulse.

You never have to prove anyone wrong; you only have to prove yourself right. Whoa...wait just a minute! That sounded pretty heavy. We HAVE to name that one. Yeah, you guessed it; "The Grand Theory about Negotiation #2." You never have to prove anyone wrong; you only have to prove yourself right. That's going in a frame and on a wall somewhere.

So, what do they do with people's reason if not argue? Well, George tried the opposite.

The opposite of hitting an injured worker with a cooperation hammer to get them to give in from the pain is to simply acknowledge where they are coming from. Awesome examiners use the tool of acknowledgement to gain cooperation and save time.

Acknowledgement: The real power tool.

Yes, the cooperation hammer is a pretty good tool, and as a matter of fact in some cases it might be the right one. But Acknowledgement is what we refer to as a "power tool." A power tool does the same job as the original tool, but much more effectively and efficiently. The power tool that can change the way an injured worker feels is Acknowledgement.

In the event you are trying to be persuasive, the first two steps are pretty clear. The first is to ask the question "Why", and the second one is to "Acknowledge" the injured worker's point of view.

An important maxim (a maxim is a truth to be held) is: "People will consider what you have to say; to the exact degree you demonstrate you understand their point of view." Let's call this "Carl's Cooperation Maxim."

Through the years of observing interactions, we've found this to be very true. People will consider what you have to say to the exact degree you demonstrate you understand their point of view. Let's take a look at this.

In the previous example, the examiner clearly started an argument by pulling out the cooperation hammer and whacking away at an injured worker who didn't want to fill out the form. Watch how the tempo of the conversation changes, if the examiner uses the right tool.

Teresa George knew how to use this tool. Today she is a wine maker, but at one time she was an awesome examiner. Here is how she would have handled it:

Teresa: Mr. Wimsatt, in order for me continue your disability benefits, you need to complete the form I sent you and send it back to me.

Mr. Wimsatt: I'm not doing that, no way.

Teresa: Can I ask why?

Mr. Wimsatt: Because I'm tired of you guys making me jump through hoops. Why should I run around doing your job? I'm the one who got injured. I'm the victim.

Teresa: Mr. Wimsatt, if you don't want to fill out the paper work, because you are feeling like you are being made to jump through hoops, and feeling like a victim, I can understand that, that's reasonable. No one likes to jump through hoops, and certainly no one likes to feel like a victim.

Notice what Teresa did in this case. She completely reduced the person's anger by acknowledging it. Notice she did not agree with it and she did not say "Yes, you are right, you are a victim." She simply acknowledged where the person was coming from. She called the injured worker a reasonable person. He's reasonable for the way he feels. The fact that Teresa took the time to tell this injured worker that he was a reasonable person for the way he feels is going to turn this person's feelings around.

Now, the more closely Teresa connects what she wants the injured worker to do with the way he feels, the more likely he will do it. Watch how Teresa uses this tool and returns the conversation to the facts.

CHAPTER 5

Don't Want to Fight

I don't want to fight. I'm a little bit wrong,
you're a little bit right.
You know that it's true. It's a little bit me;
it's a little bit you.

"A Little Bit Me, A Little Bit You" – The Monkeys

STEPS TO GAINING   **1. WHY**
COOPERATION: **2. ACKNOWLEDGE**
                              3. FACTS

Teresa: *Mr. Wimsatt, if you don't want to fill out the paper work, because you are feeling like you are being made to jump through hoops, and feeling like a victim, I can understand that, that's reasonable. No one likes to jump through hoops, and certainly no one likes to feel like a victim.*

If there was a way to extend your benefits without the form, so you wouldn't have to feel like you are jumping through hoops, I would love to do that for you. The truth is, it is mandatory, and not up to discretion.

I'll tell you what though. If you are able to complete the paper work, some good things will happen. Number one, you won't have to deal with this issue anymore. Number two, I will be able to extend your benefits as you are requesting. Number three, once your benefits are extended, maybe you won't have to feel like a victim anymore, because that's a lousy way to feel and I'd like to help. Would you be willing to complete the form so that I can help you?

Notice how Teresa in this case ties in this person changing the way he feels, to what she wants him to do. Once the injured worker does what Teresa wants him to do, he won't have to feel like a victim anymore. Teresa actually heard what the person said about feeling like a victim and used it to her advantage.

The idea of acknowledgement is extremely important. The best communicators use it often. Rather than trying to convince someone they're wrong, it's much easier to convince them you understand where they are coming from. Remember our maxim: people will consider what you have to say to the exact degree you demonstrate you understand their point of view.

Here's a non-claims example to help demonstrate this point. Pretend we have twin sisters named Diann and Debra.

Debra is at a conference in Las Vegas. Her sister Diann is coming out to meet her the next day, but isn't able to locate an available room. Diann is about to get on a plane to Vegas, so she calls Debra for some help.

> Diann: *Can you help me get a room for the conference tomorrow? I was not able to find one and I have to head to the airport.*
>
> Debra: *Sure I"ll call right now.*
>
> Debra: (Calls the reservation line at the hotel where she is staying) *My twin sister is coming out tonight, can I make a reservation for her?*
>
> Reservations: *No problem, we've got plenty of rooms, we're not even one-third booked. Just bring your sister in tonight and they'll be sure to get a room. You don't need to make a reservation.*
>
> After Debra picks up Diann at the airport, they arrive at the hotel and go to the registration counter.
>
> Debra: *Hello, this is my sister Diann and she needs a room for tonight.*

Jacob: (Front Desk clerk): *I'm sorry, we're completely booked.*

Debra: *But the hotel reservations person said there would be no problem.*

Jacob: (Turning the terminal around and pointing to the screen) *Madame, we have no more rooms,* (as if to say, "Look at the undisputed evidence, there are no rooms, you idiot.")

Debra: *I want to speak to the manager.*

Jacob: *Okay, hey Nicole, THIS LADY wants to talk to you.*

Nicole: *Yes, may I help you?*

Debra: *Yes, this is my twin sister. I called the 800 number this morning and asked to make a reservation. They told me they had plenty of rooms, and there would be no problem. Now I've picked her up at the airport and we are standing here and we are being told you have no rooms. I feel bad for my sister because now she is out of a room. That's just not right! Why was I told there were plenty of rooms?*

Nicole pauses for a moment, then replies: *Oh, Madame I'm so sorry. I'm sorry for the difficult situation you've been put in. I see by looking at our screen that we really don't have any rooms; the person you were talking to at the 800 number must have been looking at the wrong screen, because we have been booked for over a week. There is a huge convention in town, which is probably why your sister couldn't find a room before. I'm sorry for your inconvenience. I understand the difficulty you are going through, and I understand the position you are in, especially given the promise you made to your twin. Believe me, if we had a room right now, I would give it to your sister. I really would. The truth is, I just don't have a room to actually give. I would if I could, I just can't. Can I help you find a room somewhere else?*

Now who, of these two people that told Debra no, would Debra trust the most? Jacob, who threw the facts in her face or Nicole, who said she understood where Debra was coming from? Notice how Nicole tactfully got back to the facts. She didn't beat Debra to death with the facts, but she got her to consider the facts by acknowledging her point of view.

The idea here is to use acknowledgement as a way to get someone to believe what you are about to say. What are you acknowledging? You're acknowledging that the other person is a reasonable person for their beliefs or for their circumstance. You are not saying you agree with them, you are not saying they are right, you're simply saying that you understand where they are coming from. They are reasonable for their beliefs.

Let's apply these steps to another situation. Sarah Holton is great at this. Sarah is an assistant Vice President at one of the world's largest international insurance companies. But once upon a time, she was a claims handler.

> Sarah: *Mr. Dudenhofer, in order to get your medical bills, you're going to need to fill out this form.*
>
> Mr. Dudenhofer: *I don't want to do that.*
>
> Sarah: *Oh, can I ask why?*
>
> Mr. Dudenhofer: *Yeah, because I was told I wouldn't have to sign anything.*

Now at this point, the vast majority of people would say, "Who told you that?" That is because we are just dying to prove this person wrong. Sarah knows it doesn't matter who said it, or even what was really said. Sarah knows that most of the time, people's reasons for not cooperating has nothing to do with the issue at hand. She knows that great negotiators never argue with reasons, they argue the facts. So, here is what Sarah says:

Sarah: *Mr. Dudenhofer, if you don't want to fill out this Medical Authorization because you were told you wouldn't have to sign anything, I understand that, that's reasonable. Who ever told you that was mistaken, and I am very sorry about that. I don't know why you were told that. Maybe they were just trying to reassure you nothing would happen without your permission, I really don't know. The truth is; I'd like you to fill out this form so I can get your medical bills paid. If you can fill out this form and return it to me, I will do every-thing I can to make sure I get everything I need to process your claim. But again, I do understand that you were given the wrong information and I am sorry. Would you be willing to fill out these forms so I can help you?*

Did that sound better? Is it possible that this person might be a little bit more cooperative right now?

He's not going to sit there and say, "Oh boy, am I glad I got the wrong information now, thank you!" But you know what? He's a little more satisfied; he's a little calmer. He has been treated with respect and most importantly, his feelings have been acknowledged as reasonable.

He is much more open to change than he would have been if Sarah had argued with him. And at the very least, even if he stays irritated, at least he won't be irritated at Sarah. And he'll probably cooperate with her and just be irritated at somebody else.

Knowing Sarah, she might have even added, "If you know who you spoke to, I can let them know that whatever they did tell you, it might have been confusing, so we don't confuse anybody else in the future."

Can it sometimes impress someone that you will go out of your way to solve a problem? Even if they got caught in it this time, the fact that you're willing to go out of your way to solve it for the next time, can be very impressive. But the overall tool of acknowledging where someone is coming from is a very high-powered tool and one that an Awesome Examiner will have at his/her disposal at all times.

CHAPTER 6

Not Some Monster

*Marilyn Manson's real name isn't even
Marilyn Manson.
He's a skinny long haired public high
school kid from Florida,
Not some monster from out of this world.*

"The Ballad of the Kingsmen" – Todd Snider

Uncooperative people are not monsters. They are not the enemy. Sometimes they just need some help seeing the light.

A great cartoon by the name of "Non Sequitur," shows a guy with a sign saying, "The facts as they are." He's facing another guy with a sign that says, "The truth as I see it" and the line underneath reads "The irresistible force meets the immovable object."

Normally, we are "the facts as they are." The uncooperative person is the "truth as I see it." If we get in a fight, who will win? Well, usually we will win. We have the hammer. We have the facts. We can usually pound this person into submission. But that's not the point. The point is, maybe we can get this person to see the facts as they are, and maybe they will join us. After all, it's their cooperation we are after, not to win a fight.

Let's see if we can go through some more examples of gaining cooperation using the ASK – ACKNOWLEDGE – FACTS model. No wait! We'd better name it; how about, "The 3 Steps to Cooperation" model?

In all of these examples, you will see three versions. The first is where we don't even ask the person "Why?" The second is where we ask the person "Why?" but then try to prove the person wrong. And the third is where we ask "Why?" then acknowledge their reasons, and then get back to providing the facts.

Tana and Gary

Tana works at TPA as an examiner. Gary is an injured worker. Somewhere in their initial conversation, Tana realizes that Gary does not want to cooperate.

Version 1

> Tana: *Okay, all I need you to do now is fill out the medical authorization form we sent you, sign it, and send it back to me so I can get busy getting your medical bills together and request payment for your mileage and co-pays.*

Gary: *I'm not doing that.*

Tana: *You don't want to fill it out or sign it?*

Gary: *Both.*

Tana: *Then we can't get your bills paid.* (Whack!)

That is pretty much how most conversations progress.

Version 2

Tana: *Okay, all I need you to do now is fill out the medical authorization form we sent you, sign it, and send it back to me so I can get busy getting your medical bills together and request payment for your mileage and co-pays.*

Gary: *I'm not doing that.*

Tana: *You don't want to fill it out or sign it?*

Gary: *Both.*

Tana: *Can you tell me why?*

Gary: *Sure. Because I talked to my neighbor, and he's in his second year of law school, and he said, "Don't sign anything."*

Tana: *Well, your neighbor doesn't know our process for processing medical bills. You will need to fill out the authorization forms.*

Notice how Tana jumps directly to try to prove Gary wrong. It's natural for us to want to show someone they are wrong. But if Tana tries this, she will fail. You see, if she attacks the neighbor in any way, she will automatically lose credibility, because the injured worker already trusts his neighbor much more than he trusts Tana. Also keep in mind, if Tana says anything to disparage the neighbor, even though she isn't really attacking the neighbor, she is really attacking Gary for relying on his neighbor. She is literally trying to get Gary to admit that listening to his neighbor was dumb. This is not a favorable strategy for Tana.

Tana should remember three important things:

1. People will consider what you have to say; to the exact degree you demonstrate you understand their point of view.

2. Great negotiators never argue with reasons; they argue the facts.

3. You never have to prove anyone wrong; you only have to prove yourself right.

Version 3

Tana: Okay, all I need you to do now is fill out the medical authorization form we sent you, sign it, and send it back to me so I can get busy getting your medical bills together and request payment for your mileage and co-pays.

Gary: I'm not doing that.

Tana: You don't want to fill it out or sign it?

Gary: Both.

Tana: Can you tell me why?

Gary: Sure. Because I talked to my neighbor, and he's in his second year of law school, and he said, "Don't sign anything."

Tana: Gary, if you talked to your neighbor, and he is someone you trust and you respect his opinion, and he told you not to sign anything, then I can understand why you wouldn't want to sign the form. That's reasonable; that makes sense. This form, allows us to get your medical bills so we CAN get you paid. That is the purpose of this form. If you'll sign the form, I'll get busy gathering your bills and make sure they all get paid. Would you sign the form so I can help you?

Now, maybe Gary will sign the form, and maybe he won't. But the highest probability is he is much more likely to cooperate with someone who understands his point by acknowledging his reasons than someone who whacks him with the cooperation hammer.

Christine and Scott

Christine is an examiner for an insurance company. Scott has just received his initial contact from Christine, and she is trying to get a complete medical history from him. Christine is a busy person who doesn't have time for a lot of nonsense.

Version 1

Christine: *Okay sir, what I am going to need to do is create a complete medical history on you. Sir, can you give me a detailed description of any medical operations you have had in the past?*

Scott: *Well, I'd really rather not get into that.*

Christine: *You don't want to answer the question?*

Scott: *No, not really.*

Christine: *Well, if you don't, we will have to block the provisions, benefits and settlement of the claim.* (Whack!)

Again, that is pretty much how most conversations would go. Scott will either give in and feel like he's been beaten up, or he'll lose his benefits, or start filing complaints.

Version 2

Christine: *Okay sir, what I am going to need to do is create a complete medical history on you. Sir, can you give me a detailed description of any medical operations you have had in the past?*

Scott: *Well, I'd really rather not get into that.*

Christine: *You don't want to answer the question?*

Scott: *No, not really.*

Christine: *Would you be able to tell me why?*

Scott: *Well, yeah, you see I had kind of an embarrassing operation a few years ago and I would really rather not let that information out.*

Christine: *Okay, but we have to have the information.*

Scott: *Well, like I said, it's kind of an embarrassing operation. It's kind of a delicate matter so I'd really rather not discuss it.*

Christine: *Maybe so, but we still need the information. I need to get your complete medical history so that the doctor can review your condition and provide the appropriate treatment. We can't make an exception for you or else we would have to make an exception for everybody.*

Scott: *Like I said, it's just something I'd really rather not talk about.*

Christine: *You're going to have to or else we cannot proceed with your claim. Do you want to continue with your benefits? (Whack!)*

Scott: *Well, yes of course.*

Christine: *Then you're going to have to supply me with the information.*

Scott: *Alright, alright, fine!*

Notice how Christine jumped right into arguing with Scott's reasons. Christine should remember three important things:

1. People will consider what you have to say; to the exact degree you demonstrate you understand their point of view.

2. Great negotiators never argue with reasons; they argue the facts.

3. You never have to prove anyone wrong; you only have to prove yourself right.

Version 3

Christine: *Okay sir, what I am going to need to do is create a complete medical history on you. Sir, can you give me a detailed description of any medical operations you have had in the past?*

Scott: *Well, I'd really rather not get into that.*

Christine: *You don't want to answer the question?*

Scott: *No, not really.*

Christine: *Would you be able to tell me why?*

Scott: *Well, yeah, you see I had kind of an embarrassing operation a few years ago and I would really rather not let that information out.*

Christine: *You know what Scott, if you had an embarrassing operation a couple years ago and you would rather not go over that information now because that's a delicate subject for you,*

I certainly understand that. Of course, you are entitled to your privacy and I understand that you don't want to be embarrassed. That's certainly reasonable.

I just want to let you know that my goal is not to embarrass you. My goal is to do a complete medical history on you so that we can provide the doctor with the information about your condition so that he can provide appropriate treatment. First of all, I probably won't have to get into any specific details about the operation. But even if I do, I want to let you know that I am going to treat this professionally because you are entitled to that.

So will Scott cooperate now? He may or he may not. But once again, he is more likely to cooperate with someone who shows him the respect of considering his point of view.

Court and Tiffany

Court works as an examiner. Tiffany is an injured worker who doesn't want to go to the doctor assigned by Court.

Version 1

Court: *Okay Tiffany, I understand that you have been missing your appointments with Dr. Killjoy. It is important for you to keep those appointments.*

Tiffany: *I don't want to see him anymore.*

Court: *Well, if you don't, then we can't continue your benefits.* (Whack!)

This is a pretty common reaction.

Version 2

Court: *Okay Tiffany, I understand that you have been missing your appointments with Dr. Killjoy. It is important for you to keep those appointments.*

Tiffany: *I don't want to see him anymore.*

Court: *Well, why not?*

Tiffany: *Because, he has cold hands, bad breath and smells.*

Court: *You are not dating the man; you're going for treatment. That doesn't make any sense.*

My advice again, is that Court should remember three important things:

1. People will consider what you have to say; to the exact degree you demonstrate you understand their point of view.

2. Great negotiators never argue with reasons; they argue the facts.

3. You never have to prove anyone wrong; you only have to prove yourself right.

Version 3

Court: *Okay Tiffany, I understand that you have been missing your appointments with Dr. Killjoy. It is important for you to keep those appointments.*

Tiffany: *I don't want to see him anymore.*

Court: *Well, why not?*

Tiffany: *Because, he has cold hands, bad breath and smells.*

Court: *You know, Tiffany, if you don't want to see Dr. Killjoy anymore because of his cold hands and hygiene, I understand that. I am sorry you have experienced that.*

What is important to understand is that for you to continue to see the doctor is the only way to continue your benefits. If not Dr. Killjoy, it will need to be somebody else in our network. Changing doctors is an option, but it will mean getting to know someone new and starting over in getting them up to speed on your treatment.

Your concerns are certainly valid, and I know that your benefits are very important to you, and I don't want you to lose them over this issue. Do you want a different doctor?

Tiffany: No, forget it. I'll just put up with it.

Once again, in this last version, did you see how Court took the time to acknowledge the reasons and skillfully return to the facts at hand?

Another common problem is examiners not recognizing when the time to fight is over; when the battle has already been won. The ability to recognize when the time to fight is over is just as important as winning the fight. Let's take a look at that next.

CHAPTER 7

Trust Abounding

Harmony and understanding,
sympathy and trust abounding.
No more falsehoods or derisions.
Golden living dreams of visions.
Mystic crystal revelation and the mind's true liberation.

"The Age of Aquarius" – The Fifth Dimension (Hair)

Recognizing a gift when you get it

Imagine a conversation between an examiner, Sabrina and an injured worker, Jennifer.

> Jennifer: *I want to make sure my husband is compensated for the time he has taken off of work to just be home with me.*

> Sabrina: *I am sorry Jennifer, we can't do that.*

> Jennifer: *That's not fair. He's been so helpful and he deserves something.*

Sabrina: *I understand that. It's just that those are not expenses that can be paid under the workers' comp guidelines.*

Jennifer: *But I really, really think he should get something!*

Sabrina: *I do understand. If there was a way to pay for something like that, I would love to do it. The guidelines simply to not allow it.*

Jennifer: *That's a rip off!*

Sabrina: *It's not a rip off. If we paid something like that, then people could claim payment for their whole family sitting at home.*

Jennifer: *I would never do anything like that!*

Sabrina: *I'm not saying you would, but some people would. So that's why it isn't paid.*

Jennifer: *I still think that's a rip off!*

Sabrina: *Not really. This is the rule. We could easily get ripped off by some people, and we are just trying to protect ourselves. That makes sense doesn't it?*

Jennifer: *It doesn't make sense to me, because now my husband is out of two weeks' salary!*

Sabrina: *Well, no one made him stay home with you, did they?*

Jennifer: (getting upset) *No, but he was just try-ing to be nice. That's important, isn't' it?*

Sabrina: *At least you got some time alone with your husband. Doesn't that make you feel better?*

Jennifer: (Getting angrier) *It doesn't make me feel better at all. All I feel is that not only am I injured, but no one gives a damn!*

You can see that this conversation is only going to get worse. The reason it's going to get worst is because Sabrina didn't realize she already had the battle won a long time ago. Remember back when the Jennifer said, "What a rip off!" Most people would have inter-preted that as a snide comment, but the lesson for the Awesome Examiner is to recognize that as the gift. Do you know what that person is saying, when they say, "What a rip off!" Think about it just for one second, what are they really saying?

Believe it or not, what this person just said is . . . "I believe you." That's right. What this person just said is that they believe you. They're not happy about it, which is why they make the comment that it is a rip off, but nevertheless they do believe what you are telling them. There's no way for them to conclude that it's a rip off, unless they believe you first. If they didn't believe you, they'd keep arguing with you about whether or not it's really going to happen.

At this point, Sabrina should recognize that she has convinced Jennifer and stopped all fighting. Fighting is not necessary. You don't need to inflict more pain on this person. You don't need to start an argument; this person already believes you. All you have to do from this point is empathize. You have to recognize gifts when you get them. And believe it or not, this snide comment is a gift. Take it for what it is.

Imagine the conversation going slightly differently.

> Jennifer: *I want to make sure my husband is compensated for the time he has taken off of work to just be home with me.*
>
> Sabrina: *I am sorry Jennifer, we can't do that.*
>
> Jennifer: *That's not fair. He's been so helpful and he deserves something.*
>
> Sabrina: *I understand that. It's just that those are not expenses that can be paid under the workers' comp guidelines.*
>
> Jennifer: *But I really, really think he should get something!*

Sabrina: *I do understand. If there was a way to pay for something like that, I would love to do it. The guidelines simply to not allow it.*

Jennifer: *That's a rip off!*

Sabrina: *Jennifer, I understand it feels like a rip off. I appreciate that you are frustrated by the rules, and I wish it could be different. Is there something else I can help you with?*

Jennifer: *No, never mind.*

What's important to understand is that Jennifer is not going to be thrilled. She's not happy that her husband gets nothing, but at the very least, we avoid picking a fight with Sabrina. Believe it or not, because this person got treated with respect, they just may accept it even though they didn't get what they wanted, and that's one of the important things to understand about good service.

Here's Where the Story Ends

It's that little souvenir, of a colorful year,
which makes me smile inside.
Surprise, surprise, surprise, surprise, surprise.
Here's where the story ends.

"Here's Where the Story Ends" – The Sundays

Awesome Examiners have great interpersonal skills that allow them to gain cooperation from injured workers by focusing on how to help them instead of hitting them with the cooperation hammer. They know how to avoid arguments by listening to what the individual has to say and responding to their concerns. They know their credibility comes from understanding the person's point of view, not from the facts.

- Great negotiators never argue with reasons; they argue the facts!
- You never have to prove anyone wrong; you only have to prove yourself right.

- People will consider what you have to say; to the exact degree you demonstrate you understand their point of view.

Professional Copy and Subpoena Services

Debra Hinz is the Southern California Manager for Macro-Pro Copy and Subpoena Services, and can assist with all copy and subpoena needs. She also offers classes on how to obtain Kaiser records faster, bullet-proof authorization forms, and how to increase business for law firms.

Debra also puts on several workers' comp seminars each year. If you would like to find out more, or receive information on them, please feel free to contact her.

www.Macropro.com

760-613-4409

Debra.Hinz@yahoo.com

www.linkedin.com/in/debrahinz

Professional Speaking Services

Carl Van is a professional national speaker having delivered presentations throughout the U.S., Canada and the U.K.

His presentation style is upbeat, fast paced and always generates audience participation. He has received numerous recognitions throughout the years, including Most Dynamic Speaker at the national ACE conference.

Mr. Van is qualified to speak on virtually any subject regarding employee performance and customer interaction. Just a few of his Guest Speaking titles include:

General

- Awesome Claims Customer Service: You're Good. You Can Get Better
- How to Avoid Losing Customers
- The Claims Customer Service Standards: 5 Things to Never Forget

- Practical Claims Negotiations: Stop Arguing and Start Agreeing
- Real Life Time Management for Claims
- Stress Management: Give Yourself a Break Before You Die
- Improving your Attitude and Initiative
- Getting People's Cooperation – A Few Easy Steps
- What Customers Hate – And Why We Do It
- If You Can't Say it Simply and Clearly, Then You Don't Know What You're Talking About: Some Business Writing Basics
- Empathy: The Power Tool of Customer Service
- Why Are They Calling Me? Things to do to Reduce Nuisance Calls
- Let Me Do My Job: Simple Steps to get People to be Patient and Let You Do Your Job
- Trust Me: Effective Ways to Gain Credibility
- Saying No: The Right Way (and easy way), or The Wrong Way (the hard way)
- Claims Listening Skills: How to Avoid Missing the Point
- Teamwork for Claims: Ways to Reduce the Work Created by Individualism

Management

- Handling Your Difficult Employees (Without Threats and Violence)
- Teaching and Coaching for Claims Supervisors and Managers

- Initiative: How to Develop it in Your Staff
- Stop Wasting Your Time – Practical Time Management for Managers
- Effective Delegation: Why People Hate It When You Delegate, and How to Change That
- Managing Change
- Interviewing and Hiring Exceptional Claims Performers
- Motivating Your Team
- How to Make Sure Your Employees get the Most out of Training
- Inspiring Employees to Improve Themselves

For a free DVD, please visit
www.CarlVan.org or call 504-393-4570.

"Like" Carl Van on
www.Facebook.com/CarlVanSpeaker for updates.

Follow Carl Van on
www.Twitter.com/CarlVanSpeaker

In-Person Training Services

Carl Van is President & CEO of International Insurance Institute, Inc. which delivers high quality claims training directly to customers at their locations. He is the author of over 75 technical and soft skill courses that have been delivered to over 100,000 employees throughout the U.S, Canada and the U.K.

Just a few titles of his programs include:

Employee Soft-Skill

- Real-Life Time Management for Claims
- The 8 Characteristics of the Awesome Adjuster
- Claims Negotiation Training
- Conflict Resolution
- Awesome Claims Customer Service
- Managing the Telephone
- Attitude & Initiative Training for the Employee
- Empathy & Listening Skills for Claims
- Employee Organization – Managing the Desk
- Prepare for Promotion – Employee Leadership Training

- Teamwork Basics – No Employee is an Island
- Interpersonal Skills – Improving Team Member Relations
- Effective Recorded Statements
- Business Writing Skills for Employees
- Beating Anxiety and Dealing with Anger – Help for the New Employee

Manager Soft-Skill

- Time Management for Claims Supervisors and Managers
- Coaching and Teaching for Claims Supervisors and Managers
- Keys to Effective Presentations
- Teaching Your Employees the 8 Characteristics of Awesome Employees
- Motivating Your Team
- Handling Difficult Employees
- The New Supervisor
- Interviewing and Hiring Exceptional Claims Performers
- Delegation Training for Supervisors and Managers
- Managing Change
- Team Training
- Leadership Skills for Claims Supervisors and Managers
- Preparing Effective Performance Appraisals
- Managing the Highly Technical Employee

For more information and a free catalog of
courses, please visit www.InsuranceInstitute.com
or call 504-393-4570.

On-Line Training Services

Carl Van is President and owner of the Claims Education On Line website that delivers high quality claims training through streaming video that employees can access anywhere in the world.

He is also available to write, direct and present training courses specific to an individual company or industry. He wrote and presented a claims customer service course on DVD for a national company which was rolled out to all 18,000 line employees.

He is the designer, author and presenter of four on-line claims video training courses:

- Exceptional Claims Customer Service
- Negotiation Skills for the Claims Professional
- Real-Life Time Management for Claims
- Critical Thinking for Claims

For more information, visit
www.ClaimsEducationOnLine.com.

Educational Articles by Carl Van

Carl Van is owner and publisher of Claims Education Magazine, and is the author of numerous articles that have appeared in various periodicals.

Just a sample of articles written by Carl Van:

Van, Carl "Gaining Cooperation."

Weekly Article Magazine. www.WeeklyArticle.com March 2011.

Industrial Supply Magazine. www.industrialsupplymagazine.com; March, 2011.

Furniture World Magazine. www.Furnifo.com March 2011.

Contact Professional. www.ContactProfessional.com March 2011.

Promotional Consultants Today. www.PromotionalConsultantToday.org March, 2011.

Van, Carl "Three Maxims for Successful Negotiation." Dealer Marketing Magazine www.DealerMarketing. com March 2011.

Van, Carl. "Our Life's Work." Property Casualty 360. www.PropertyCasualty360.com January, 2011.

Van, Carl. "The Five Standards of Great Claims Organizations." Property Casualty 360. www. PropertyCasualty360.com February, 2011.

Van, Carl. "Online Claims Training Program Expands: Time Management for Claims added to curriculum." Claims Education Magazine. www.claimseducation-magazine.com Fall 2010.

Van, Carl. "5th Annual Claims Education Conference Earns Superbowl Status." Claims Education Magazine. Summer 2010: Pg. 1.

Van, Carl. "While Others Wait, Bold Companies Invest in Training." Subrogator. Winter 2010: Pg. 102.

Van, Carl. "While Others Wait, Bold Companies Invest in Training Part III." Claims Education Magazine. Spring 2010: Pg. 1.

Van, Carl. "While Others Wait, Bold Companies Invest in Training Part II." Claims Education Magazine. December 2009- Vol. 6, No. 6: Pg. 1.

Van, Carl. "While Others Wait, Some Invest in Training." Claims Education Magazine. October/November 2009- Vol. 6, No. 5: Pg. 3

Van, Carl. "Tips on Taking Statements & Information Gathering." Claims Education Magazine. October/ November 2009- Vol. 6, No. 5: Pg. 1.

Van, Carl. "Placing the Bets." Claims Education Magazine. March/April 2009- Vol. 6, No. 2: Pg. 1.

Van, Carl. "Lesson in Customer Service & Attitude." Claims Education Magazine. January/February 2009- Vol. 6, No. 1: Pg. 1.

Van, Carl. "Saying It the Right Way." Claims Education Magazine. Fall 2008- Vol. 5, No. 4: Pg. 8.

Van, Carl. "Critical Thinking Part Three." Claims Education Magazine. Summer 2008- Vol. 5, No. 3: Pg. 4.

Van, Carl. "Critical Thinking Part Two." Claims Education Magazine. Spring 2008- Vol. 5, No. 2: Pg. 4.

Van, Carl. "Critical Thinking Part One." Claims Education Magazine. Winter 2008- Vol. 5, No. 1: Pg. 4.

Van, Carl. "Desire for Excellence." Claims Education Magazine. Fall 2007- Vol. 4, No. 4: Pg. 14.

Van, Carl. "Building a Claim Team." Claims. October 2005.

Van, Carl. "In Search of Initiative." Claims. September 2005.

Van, Carl. "A Velvet Hammer Can Expedite Negotiations." Claims Education Magazine. Summer 2005- Vol. 1, No. 1: Pg. 10.

Van, Carl. "Claims Management: Desire for Excellence." Claims. July 2005.

Van, Carl. "Empathizing with Customers." Claims. June 2005.

Van, Carl. "Never Stop Learning." Claims. May 2005.

Van, Carl. "Interpersonal Skills: Avoid the Hammer." Claims. April 2005.

Van, Carl. "Secrets of Successful Time Management." Claims. March 2005.

Van, Carl. "Attitude." Claims Magazine. February 2005: Pg. 10.

Van, Carl. "Tend to Your Garden: A Vision of Claims Education." Claims. February 2003: Pg. 34.

Van, Carl. "Adjusters: How not to Drive Away Clients." National Underwriter. September 24, 2001.

Van, Carl & Sue Tarrach. "The 8 Characteristics of Awesome Adjusters." Claims. December 1996.

Carl Van is available for consulting, training and guest speaking appearances. To contact Mr. Van, call 504-393-4570 or visit:

www.CarlVan.org

www.Facebook.com/CarlVanSpeaker

www.Linkedin.com/CarlVan (Carl Van - Awesome Adjuster group)

Articles Featuring Carl Van

Mr. Van has been the subject of numerous articles outlining his services and educational philosophy. A few are:

Gilkey, Eric. "Strategies for Gaining Cooperation." IASIU. Monday, September 13, 2010: Pg. 4.

Henry, Susan, and Mary Anne Medina. "Evaluating Adjuster Performance." Claims. August 2010: Pg. 36.

Gilkey, Eric. "Hiring and Motivating the Right People." NASP Daily News, November 3, 2009: Pg. 6.

"Permission to Say, 'I'm Sorry." Canadian Underwriter. September 1, 2008.

Aznoff, Dan. "Fair Oaks Students Take Speaker's Advice to Heart for Positive Attitude." The Sacramento Bee. April 12, 2007: City Section, Pg. G5.

Friedman, Sam. "WC Claimants 'Not the Enemy,' Trainer says." National Underwriter. September 24, 2001.

Prochaska, Paul. "Awesome Adjusting Revisited: A Return to Customer Service." <u>Claims.</u> February, 2000.

Hays, Daniel. "Being Kinder and Gentler Pays Off: Insurance Claims is a Customer Service Business." <u>Claims.</u> December 2000: Pg. 56.

Carl Van is available for consulting, training and guest speaking appearances. To contact Mr. Van, call 504-393-4570 or visit:

<u>www.CarlVan.org</u>

<u>www.Facebook.com/CarlVanSpeaker</u>

<u>www.Linkedin.com/CarlVan</u> (Carl Van - Awesome Adjuster group)

Books by Carl Van

Van, Carl. <u>The 8 Characteristics of the Awesome Adjuster</u>. Published by Arthur Hardy Enterprises, Inc., ISBN 0-930892-66-6 (Metairie, LA) Copyright © 2005

Van, Carl. <u>Gaining Cooperation: Some Simple Steps to Getting Customers to do What You Want Them to do</u>. Published by International Insurance Institute, Inc., ISBN 1456334107 & 13-9781456334109 (New Orleans, LA) Copyright © 2011

Van, Carl. <u>Attitude, Ability and the 80-20 Rule</u>. Published by International Insurance Institute, Inc., (New Orleans, LA) Copyright © 2011

Coming Soon:

Van, Carl and Hinz, Debra. <u>Gaining Cooperation: 3 Easy Steps to Getting Injured Workers to do What you Want Them to do</u>. Published by International Insurance Institute, Inc., (New Orleans, LA) Copyright © 2011

Van, Carl and Wimsatt, Laura. <u>The Claims Cookbook: A Culinary Guide to Job Satisfaction.</u> Published by International Insurance Institute, Inc., (New Orleans, LA) Copyright © 2011

Van, Carl. <u>Hiring Excellent Employees – Givers vs. Takers</u>. Published by International Insurance Institute, Inc., (New Orleans, LA) Copyright © 2011

Van, Carl. <u>Critical Thinking for the Claims Professional.</u> Published by International Insurance Institute, Inc., (New Orleans, LA) Copyright © 2011

Van, Carl. <u>The 8 Characteristics of the Awesome Employee</u>. To be published in 2012.

Carl Van is available for consulting, training and guest speaking appearances. To contact Mr. Van, call 504-393-4570 or visit:

<u>www.CarlVan.org</u>

<u>www.Facebook.com/CarlVanSpeaker</u>

<u>www.Linkedin.com/CarlVan</u> (Carl Van - Awesome Adjuster group)

Contact Carl Van

Carl Van is available for consulting, training and guest speaking appearances. To contact Mr. Van, call 504-393-4570 or find him at any of the following:

www.CarlVan.org

www.Facebook.com/CarlVanSpeaker

www.Linkedin.com/CarlVan (Carl Van – Awesome Adjuster group)

www.Twitter.com/CarlVanSpeaker

www.ClaimsEducationMagazine.com

www.ClaimsEducationConference.com

www.ClaimsExecutiveAcademy.com

www.ClaimsManagerAcademy.com

www.ClaimsSkillsAcademy.com

www.ClaimsProfessionalBooks.com

www.ClaimsEducationOnLine.com

www.InsuranceInstitute.com

Made in the USA
Columbia, SC
16 February 2020